DRAW IT!

DRAW HORRIBLE PICTURES

PAUL GAMBLE

WINDMILL
BOOKS ™

NEW YORK

Published in 2015 by Windmill Books, An Imprint of Rosen Publishing
29 East 21st Street, New York, NY 10010

Copyright © Arcturus Holdings Ltd

First Edition

Text: Paul Gamble and Anna Brett

Illustrations: Paul Gamble

Design: Notion Design

Editors: Joe Harris, Anna Brett, and Samantha Hilton

With thanks to Frances Evans and Jessica Williams

Library of Congress Cataloging-in-Publication Data

Gamble, Paul, 1958-

 Draw horrible pictures / By Paul Gamble. -- First Edition.

    pages cm. -- (Draw it!)

 Includes index.

 ISBN 978-1-4777-9140-0 (library binding) -- ISBN 978-1-4777-9141-7
(pbk.) -- ISBN 978-1-4777-9142-4 (6-pack)

1. Characters and characteristics in art--Juvenile literature.
2. Drawing--Technique--Juvenile literature. I. Title.

 NC825.C43G364 2015

 741.2--dc23

                            2014008364

 Printed in the United States

 SL004211US

CPSIA Compliance Information: Batch #AS4102WM: For Further Information contact Windmill Books, New York, New York at 1-866-478-0556

CONTENTS

GETTING STARTED

This book will teach you how to draw a cast of wonderful characters. Simply follow the step-by-step instructions and get drawing!

1. Start with a plain piece of unlined paper. If you are going to paint your picture, you should use thick paper.

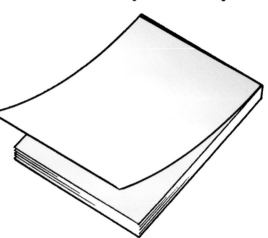

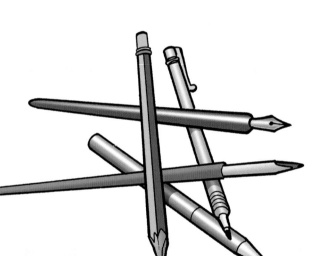

2. Use a pencil to copy the step-by-step instructions. Soft pencils are good for rough sketches. Hard pencils are best for details.

3. Draw over your pencil lines with a black pen or a thin brush and black ink. The ink must be waterproof if you are going to add watercolor paints to your picture.

INK

4. When the pen ink has dried, use a large, soft eraser to remove the pencil marks. Now your picture is looking nice and neat!

5. Complete your picture by coloring it in with colored felt-tip pens, pencils, or paint.

6. Paintbrushes come in different shapes. When painting, use a thin, pointed brush for detail and a fatter brush for flat areas of color.

HARRY HORNET

1. Harry Hornet has an oval-shaped body. The fatter end will be his head, so decide what direction you want him to face.

2. Add two wings on top of his body, and notice how the back one goes behind the body. Add his pointed stinger and nose.

3. Draw in a huge eye and a zigzag line for his mouth. You can erase the guide lines across his wings and nose now.

4. Connect Harry's nose to his mouth, and add in the second eye. Draw curved lines around his body for markings.

5. Time to add some details: eyebrows, the open mouth, and lines on his wings. A puff of air behind him shows he's flying.

6. Finish your artwork by coloring in the stripes with black and yellow, then add some veins to Harry's buzzing wings.

SPITEFUL SPIDER

1. Start with an easy circle for Spiteful Spider's body. How large are you going to draw him?

2. Add eight lines sticking out of the circle for his legs. Count to make sure you've got them all.

3. Now make the legs rounded and add two eyeballs. Spiders actually have eight eyes, so you could add another six to your drawing!

4. Time to transform him into the naughty spider he really is! Give him angry eyebrows and a wide mouth. Draw in a jagged line around his body.

5. A furry body and fangs make this a spider to steer clear of. Outline his tongue, too.

6. To finish Spiteful Spider, give him pupils and shade around his eyes. Add some hairs on his legs, then color him in black, blue, green, or purple.

SLiMY TOAD

1. To begin drawing this toad, sketch a circle, then put a sausage shape on top of it.

2. Draw arches for the outlines of his back legs and triangles for his two front feet.

3. Draw wide triangles for his back feet and add three toes on each front foot. Add two eyes, and then show where his giant mouth is going to hang. Make it huge!

4. Add toes on the back feet and then shape his mouth. I wonder how many flies he has swallowed today?

5. Now draw his long, sticky tongue flying out to catch prey. Give him some angry eyebrows, too.

6. Finish your toad by adding lots of warts and his pupils. Then color him in with green and a bright pink tongue. Don't forget to draw the poor fly!

SNOTTY SNAiL

1. Make the basic shape of Snotty Snail's body by drawing a triangle with wavy sides.

2. Draw the round head and long tail at either end. He looks like a slug without his shell!

3. Now add a soft square shape for Snotty Snail's shell, and then draw his eyes floating above his head.

4. Give him stalks for his eyes, a mouth, and a comfy cushion of slime to sit on!

5. Add a spiral to his shell, then draw the slimy trail that he has left behind.

6. Finish him by coloring in his shell and skin with muddy brown colors. Then add a nice dollop of snot dripping from his nose, some warts on his skin, and pupils going in different directions.

SMELLY JELLYFISH

1. Start off with a curved semicircle. This will be the jellyfish's large head.

2. Draw a squiggly frill across the bottom, and add two round eyes.

3. Add the beginnings of the six tentacles. Make them wavy, like hair.

4. Finish drawing the thick tentacles, and then draw a long, smiley mouth.

5. Time for the horrible part! Give him some fangs and heavy eyelids.

6. Finish the jellyfish by coloring with purple pencils, then add shading, pupils, spots, and bubbles to show that he's underwater.

CRUNCHY CROC

1. First, draw a semicircle, which will form the base of Crunchy Croc's body.

2. Draw the outline of his head and a bean shape for the start of his tail. It doesn't look much like Crunchy yet ...

3. Next, pencil in those snappy jaws. Draw the tip of his tail and four circles where his feet are going to be.

4. Time to draw in his legs and connect his tail. Erase the guide lines inside his mouth, then outline his eyes.

5. Crunchy needs angry eyebrows and claws to look scary. He's taking shape now!

6. Finish Crunchy with lots of spikes down his back and pointed teeth. Most crocs are green, but you can make Crunchy any color you like!

SNEAKY SNAKE

1. Start with a long "S" shape for Sneaky Snake's body, and add a small, round head.

2. Add his large rectangular jaw and the first coil in his squeezy trap!

3. Add a second coil and two eyes. Draw a line down his neck: This is where his back changes into his tummy.

4. Add a third coil and a wavy tongue. Add a circle to show where the monkey's hand is going to poke out.

5. Draw the final coil and finish the forked tongue. Now add the four-fingered monkey hand.

6. To finish Sneaky, choose some bright colors to shade him in, then give him pupils, nostrils, and fangs. Draw lines across his tummy, and he's ready to eat his dinner!

PINCHY CRAB

1. Begin to sketch Pinchy Crab by drawing an oval leaf shape.

2. Draw two more leaf shapes above the first one. These will be the pincers.

3. Add some arms to connect the pincers to the body, two eyes, and the tops of his legs. It looks like he is doing ballet!

4. Make the bottoms of his legs pointy, and then create his big pincers by drawing a lightning shape across the oval.

5. Thick eyebrows, shadows under his eyes, and a creepy smile turn him from a regular crab into a cunning crustacean!

6. Pinchy is almost ready. Just choose some eye-catching colors to fill him in. Then add a single tooth and pupils, and he is ready to scuttle off ... sideways, of course!

SHARKFiN

1. To draw Crunchy Croc's pal Sharkfin, start off with a fat banana shape.

2. Draw a line down the middle to show where his belly will be, put a fin on his back, and start the tail.

3. Add his smaller fins, and mark where his gaping mouth is going to be. The tail is a quarter moon shape.

4. Draw in an eye and some gills. This is the last time Sharkfin is going to look friendly.

5. Give him angry eyes, pointy teeth, and show where his tail has a battle scar from a fish fight.

6. To finish Sharkfin, color him in, then shade the inside of his mouth and around his eye, for an extra-evil glare!

SNEEZY LUiGi

1. Draw a circle, then attach the rectangular shape of Luigi's torso to it.

2. Draw the outline of his bent legs, his tissue, and a circle where his hand is going to be.

3. Add some arms and feet. He has bent legs to show the force of his sneeze!

4. Divide his legs in two, then give him some fingers and an ear. Outline his T-shirt, hair, and tissue.

5. Add in some more detail to the T-shirt and his hair, then draw triangles for your snot guide lines!

6. Finally, add extra wrinkles around Luigi's eyes to show they're squeezed shut. Don't forget to color in his clothes. Then choose a gruesome green for the flying snot!

BABY TANTRUM

1. Start by drawing a triangle with a circle sitting on top. This will help you get the baby's proportions right.

2. Within the triangle, draw an egg for the body, beans for the feet, and sausages for the arms. Feeling hungry?

3. Add circles where his hands will be. Then add legs and a big, wailing mouth.

4. Erase the triangle guide lines. Now he's taking shape. Draw fingers, ears, closed eyes, one big tooth, and a tongue.

5. Time to add detail! Add buttons and cuffs to his footie, then concentrate on his face.

6. To finish your angry baby, give him lots of nasty pimples all over his face. Then color in his clothes and choose a bright pink pencil for his mouth and zits. Tears and movement lines show he is really grumpy!

DRAWING A HORRIBLE SCENE

Now that you have learned how to draw all kinds of different horrible characters, why not bring several together to create a whole scene?

First, draw a rough sketch of your picture in pencil, using simple shapes. Then add detail. Try to fill the whole space.

Draw in some scary background figures, and add lots of gooey mud oozing slime all over your scene. We've also drawn in a skull to make it extra yucky.

Now it's time to add some color! Think about which shades work well together and how they make you feel.

We chose a dark blue for the night sky. It makes the whole picture feel a little spooky. A horrible muddy yellow color was used for the ground.

We used strong, bright colors for our characters. This helps them really stand out!

To create a sense of energy and excitement, place your characters in lots of different positions.

GLOSSARY

guide line (GYD LYN) A simple line that shows where to fill in a drawing with more lines or color.

hard pencil (HARD PEN-sul) A pencil with a hard lead that is good for making thin strokes and fine details in a drawing.

movement lines (MOOV-ment LYNZ) Lines that show motion.

rough sketch (RUF SKECH) A drawing made quickly to give an idea of the finished picture.

scene (SEEN) A picture of a place.

semicircle (SE-mee-sur-kul) Half of a circle.

soft pencil (SOFT PEN-sul) A pencil with a soft lead that is good for making thick strokes or filling in a drawing.

FURTHER READING

Emberley, Ed. *Ed Emberley's Drawing Book of Weirdos.* New York: LB Kids, 2005.

Levy, Barbara Soloff. *How to Draw Animals.* Mineola, NY: Dover Publications, 2008.

Levy, Barbara Soloff. *How to Draw Funny Monsters.* Mineola, NY: Dover Publications, 2009.

WEBSITES

For web resources related to the subject of this book, go to: www.windmillbooks.com/weblinks and select this book's title.

INDEX